Imaginative Bible Meditations

Strengthening Family Devotions with Creativity

Jenny Alexander

Jenny Alexander Publishing

Jenny Alexander

Disclaimer:

This publication is meant as a source of valuable information for the reader, however it is not meant as a substitute for expert assistance. If such level of assistance is required, the services of a competent professional should be sought.

Table of Contents

Jenny Alexander

Dedication

5

I dedicate this book to the families who will read it. I pray that your faith and bond will be strengthened as you study together.

Jenny Alexander

Introduction

"This Book of the Law shall not depart from your mouth, but you shall meditate in it day and night, that you may observe to do according to all that is written in it. For then you will make your way prosperous, and then you will have good success." JOSHUA 1:8 (NKJV)

Have you ever wanted to bring more creativity to your family's devotional times? You can, and this book will show you how.

In the chapters that follow, you'll discover new ways to meditate on the Bible that will ignite your creativity.

As you interact with this book, may the following pages strengthen your faith, your devotional time, and your family's bond.

Preface

This book was partly inspired by my husband. He encouraged me to draw Scripture during our dating days. This helped me look forward to my Bible reading time and grow as a believer.

At first I thought I could only draw stick figures, but it turned out I could draw more than that. My creativity blossomed. Despite my blossoming creativity, I was unsure about this book in the early stages. However, Paige Spear's belief in its premise encouraged me to continue and her thoughtful edits gave me more direction.

Maybe you think can't draw or lead your children in creative pursuits. On the other hand, maybe it's not that you doubt your ability to draw, write, or lead. Maybe you've lost your creativity entirely. If that's the case, then allow this book to give you permission to reconnect with your creative side while enabling your children to flourish in this area. Our lives are enriched when we express ourselves creatively.

Chapter 1

IMAGINE: A BIBLICAL WORD STUDY

Peanut butter and jelly go together. So do milk and cookies, and peas and carrots. What you may not realize is how our imaginations can complement Bible study. Allow me to convince you.

Are you familiar with biblical word studies? If not, they're most enlightening and can be done with tools like Blue Letter Bible. This is an online Bible dictionary that allows you to look up Bible words in their original language.

We're going to use Blue Letter Bible to study Psalm 1:2 (NKJV), which says: *"But his delight is in the law of the Lord, And in His law he meditates day and night."*

Specifically, we're going to focus on the word meditate. My previous understanding of this verse was that I should delight in the Scriptures and rehearse them over and over in my mind. Merriam-Webster's dictionary agrees. Their definitions include: *"to engage in contemplation or reflection; to focus one's thoughts on: reflect on or ponder over; or to plan or project in the mind: intend, purpose."*

These definitions are great, but what does Blue Letter Bible say?

The KJV translates Strong's H1897 (meditate) in the following manner: meditate (6x), mourn (4x), speak (4x), imagine (2x), study (2x), mutter (2x), utter (2x), roaring (1x), sore (1x), talk (1x).

The most striking word in this list is the word imagine. Spiritually speaking, we can imagine many things. We might imagine heaven, meeting saints of old, or the salvation of our loved ones. We might picture Bible stories in our minds. But beyond these kinds of imaginings, have you or your family ever imagined a Bible verse?

If you're wondering what that would look like, let me offer some suggestions. You could write a song or poem about what you've read. Thus, imagining how Bible verses or concepts fit into a chorus or stanza. After all, you're thinking about the Word as you do these things. Let me give you concrete examples.

I wrote a book of poems based on the Bible. A sample haiku from that book is below. The biblical references are 2 Corinthians 5:21 (NKJV) and Galatians 3:13 (NKJV).

God's Great Mercy

Jesus took God's wrath…
upon Himself on the tree.
He chose not to flee.

Similarly, my husband writes original Christian music that's intended to teach Bible principles. Check out his YouTube channel: CurtisAlexandermusic

You can also draw Scripture. I'd never heard of this, but my husband used this method to teach children at church. Go ahead and peek at the last two chapters if you want examples.

Scripture drawing is a great way to learn, especially for children. I don't know the age of yours, but kids often like to draw and colour. Teaching your family to draw and colour Bible verses can add an extra dimension to your devotional times.

This method of study could even help you memorize Scripture. When you describe something in your own words or when you draw a picture to represent what you've read, you remember it better. In other words, you've translated what you read into something easily understand understandable.

Drawing Scripture and writing poetry or music lyrics are just a few ways to mediate on or imagine the Word. I'll share other ways in the following chapters.

Reflection Questions

1. What do you think about drawing Scripture? Is this a new concept for you and your family?

2. What was your understanding of the word meditate? How would you and your family define it?

3. Would you add other examples of creative Bible meditation besides writing lyrics or poetry?

4. Have you and your family ever done a biblical word study?

5. How do you and your family usually study Scripture?

Chapter 2

THE BIBLE: A REVIEW

In this chapter, we're going to review the Bible. As you read this with your family, you're welcome to add your own insights.

Many other books are reviewed. Check Amazon for customer reviews of countless books. Since so many people review books, why don't we review the Bible?

The Bible is a collection of words, pages, and verses. It's like other books in that way, but it's unique. Countless men over hundreds of years wrote the words. Yet the voice and content are consistent throughout because the Holy Spirit inspired these men.

The Bible is a book like no other, isn't it? With a review of the Book of books as a foundation for igniting our creativity, we can lay a foundation for our meditations. We can fall in love all over again with this special book and its Author.

Let's see what the Bible says about itself.

"All Scripture is given by inspiration of God, and is profitable for doctrine, for reproof, for correction, for instruction in righteousness, that the man of God may be complete, thoroughly equipped for every good work." (2 Timothy 3:16–17, NKJV)

"Your word is a lamp to my feet And a light to my path." (Psalm 119:105, NKJV)

These verses say that we have the Bible for a reason. Other books shed light on subjects, but only the Bible makes the claims it does.

Only through the Bible are we changed from sinners to saints by believing in its message. Only the Bible restores our souls. Only the Bible is an anchor for our souls in troubled times. It's worth meditating on, and the Bible is worth trusting. We can trust what it says because God cannot lie: *"..in hope of eternal life which God, who cannot lie, promised before time began," (Titus 1:2, NKJV)*

I've heard it said that the Bible is a special history book because it's HIS story. It's Jesus' story. The Bible is about Jesus from beginning to end.

St. Augustine said, *"The New Testament is hidden in the Old Testament, and the Old Testament is revealed in the New Testament."* This is because there are many types and shadows of Jesus in the Old Testament. The New Testament reveals these shadows and types.

Did you know that Noah's Ark is a type of Jesus? We are safe from God's judgment in Jesus, just as Noah and his family were safe from God's judgment in the ark. Just as God locked Noah and his family in the ark, we are safe in Christ. Some think the Old Testament is boring, but it's not if you read it to find Jesus in its pages. Bible study never needs to be boring.

I've also heard that the Bible is God's love letter to us. The Bible shows us how God loves us. He shows His love by atoning for our sins through Jesus' perfect life, death, burial, and resurrection. The Bible shows us how to live without fear of death.

What other book makes that claim? What love God has for us to leave us the Bible, the book that tells us the truth about life and death. The Bible is the best-selling book of all time for a reason. No other book tells us the truth like it does.

Now, let's take a moment to look at some facts and statistics.

Bible Facts

Early Christians paid dearly for others to have their own Bibles.

The Matthew Bible was the second English Bible.

The Geneva Bible was the first English translation to have chapters and verses numbered.

A woman printed the Jane Aitken's Bible. That was a first!

America revised the KJV in 1901 and called it the American Standard Version.

Bible Statistics

20 million Bibles are sold each year

1.66 million Bibles are sold each month

384,615 Bibles are sold per week

54,945 Bibles are sold every day

2,289 Bibles are sold per hour

38 Bibles are sold per minute

6.4 Bibles are sold every 10 seconds

Reflection Questions

1. What is your family's favourite Bible passage or book of the Bible?

2. How many copies of the Bible do your family own? Are they the same translation or different translations?

3. What is your family's favourite translation? Are there any translations you don't like?

4. How often do you read the Bible with your family?

5. Do you prefer to read the Old Testament, the New Testament, or both? Why?

Chapter 3

AN INTERVIEW WITH JESUS

In this chapter, I show you how to "interview" Jesus or other biblical persons. In short, I did this by creating questions I knew I'd find answers to in the Bible.

I also imagined what His biography would look like if He had a Facebook or Instagram account. Jesus has many names, doesn't he? Thus, one of His biographies might read: *Founder of the earth, the heavens, the world, and its fullness.*

"The heavens are Yours, the earth also is Yours; The world and all its fullness, You have founded them." (Psalm 89:11, NKJV)

That's quite a biography, isn't it? Jesus created everything we see and we don't see. He created it all. No one who has ever lived could top Jesus - not Mark Zuckerberg or Bill Gates, not Abraham

Lincoln or Walt Disney. We serve a pretty amazing God. No one makes the claims that He does. No one has His credentials. No one is as great as He is.

Why don't you stop for a moment and take a moment to tell Him how amazing He is. Which of His attributes come to mind as you and your family praise Him?

Let's get on with the interview. Why don't we start at the beginning?

When were You created? I've always been! No one created Me. I'm the Creator of all things.

"Indeed before the day was, I am He; And there is no one who can deliver out of My hand; I work, and who will reverse it?" (Isaiah 43:13, NKJV)

What do You do for a living? I'm the Lord of lords and the King of kings. I'm also the Prince of Peace, the Mighty God, and the Counsellor. I'm the Great Physician and the Good Shepherd. If you read My book, you'll learn all about Me. I hope you will!

"These will make war with the Lamb, and the Lamb will overcome them, for He is Lord of lords and King of kings; and those who are with Him are called, chosen, and faithful." (Revelation 17:14, NKJV)

"For unto us a Child is born, Unto us a Son is given; And the government will be upon His shoulder. And His name will be called Wonderful, Counsellor, Mighty God, Everlasting Father, Prince of Peace." (Isaiah 9:6, NKJV)

When Jesus heard that, He said to them, "Those who are well have no need of a physician, but those who are sick." (Matthew 9:12, NKJV)

"I am the good shepherd. The good shepherd gives His life for the sheep." (John 10:11, NKJV)

Talk about Your body. My body is the church. I call it beloved.

1 John 4:11 (NKJV) says: *"Beloved, if God so loved us, we also ought to love one another."*

Romans 12:5 (NKJV) says: *"so we, being many, are one body in Christ, and individually members of one another."*

When we read about Your Word, what do we gain? My word is incomparable. Read it, and you'll gain more than you can imagine.vSee 2 Timothy 3:16–17 mentioned previously.

What makes You unique? My word says that there is no one alive like Me. Do you believe it?

"for at this time I will send all My plagues to your very heart, and on your servants and on your people, that you may know that there is none like Me in all the earth." (Exodus 9:14, NKJV)

Have You had any cool experiences? There are too many to write about, but a few include:

I parted the Red Sea through my servant Moses. See Exodus 14.

My Son turned water into wine at a wedding. See John 2.

My Son walked on water. So did His disciple, Peter! See Matthew 14.

Above all, My Son died on a cruel cross, was buried, and rose again for YOUR salvation. See 1 Corinthians 15:1-4 and John 3:16.

What are Your hobbies? When my Son lived among you, He was a carpenter. Mark 6:3 (NKJV) says, *"Is this not the carpenter, the Son of Mary, and brother of James, Joses, Judas, and Simon?"*

Reflection Questions

1. What questions would you ask Jesus? Make sure you can find answers to them in the Bible.

2. What do you love most about God?

3. What would you like to know about Him?

4. What 'cool experiences' would you have added?

5. Would you have added any other Scriptures to these answers? You're welcome to go through them again and add your own thoughts.

Chapter 4

THE BIBLE AND *THE THREE LITTLE PIGS*

It's time to switch gears and try another way of meditating on the Bible. In chapters 3 to 5 we'll look at three children's stories in light of Scripture, and in chapters 6 and 7 we'll see how nursery rhymes compare with the Bible.

Some time ago, I read my nieces the popular story of *The Three Little Pigs*. Imagine my surprise when it reminded me of biblical principles. This is another way to meditate. It's also a way for the natural to shed light on the spiritual.

What are the benefits of shedding spiritual light on the natural? Comparing the natural with the spiritual reminds us that there is more to life than what we see. It reminds us that as Christians, we walk by faith. We put our faith in the things we don't see rather than the things we see.

When the natural doesn't make sense, comparing it with Scripture brings understanding. This encourages and comforts us as we go through things we don't understand. It reminds us that our faith is in God and His Word.

This kind of exercise can help us through various stages of life that are confusing. It can remind us of our purpose when things are upside down and we feel directionless. Comparing the natural and the spiritual also gives us an anchor for our souls.

Now, what about you and your family? Can you think of other benefits of comparing the natural with the spiritual?

Our first comparison is with the *Three Little Pigs*. If you don't know the story, it's about three brothers who are pigs. They're building houses and each one builds his house with different materials. The first two brothers use flimsy material, but the third brother uses bricks.

The pigs have a big bad wolf for a neighbour. That wolf is disguised as a grandmother. At first, the wolf fools the pigs, but only for a short time.

Realizing their mistake, they run for cover as the wolf demolishes the first two pigs' houses. They take refuge in their brother's brick house, where they are safe from the enemy.

Now that you know the premise of the story, if you didn't already, let's move on to the biblical comparisons.

Comparison 1: Shortcuts

Two of the little pigs weren't smart. They took a shortcut and built their houses quickly, but their houses didn't last very long. The third pig took a different approach. He wasn't afraid of hard work and took his time to build a house that would last.

Matthew 7:24–27 (NKJV) says: *"Therefore whoever hears these sayings of Mine, and does them, I will liken him to a wise man who built his house on the rock: and the rain descended, the floods came, and the winds blew and beat on that house; and it did not fall, for it was founded on the rock. But everyone who hears these sayings of Mine, and does not do them, will be like a foolish man who built his house on the sand: and the rain descended, the floods came, and the winds blew and beat on that house; and it fell. And great was its fall."*

Discipline is essential in the life of a believer. Building a relationship with God takes time. We need time in His Word, in prayer, and with other believers. Our relationship with God grows through the "hard work" of discipline. And like the third pig who built a better house, our relationship with God has lasting power. John 10:28 (NKJV) tells us: *"And I give them eternal life, and they shall never perish; neither shall anyone snatch them out of My hand."*

Comparison 2: Our Way Isn't Always the Right Way

We're not always right, are we? Before we knew Christ as Saviour and Lord, we might have believed there were many ways to heaven. But the Bible tells us Jesus is the only way. John 14:6 (NKJV) says: *"Jesus said to him, "I am the way, the truth, and the life. No one comes to the Father except through Me."*

Let's think of an example of this principle in the natural. Maybe one of your children likes a popular kid at school who isn't a good influence. Though mom or dad lets the child know they don't approve of the friendship, the child continues to spend time with that person. In the end, let's imagine this leads to your child getting blamed for something the other kid did.

"Do not be unequally yoked together with unbelievers. For what fellowship has righteousness with lawlessness? And what communion has light with darkness?" (2 Corinthians 6:14, NKJV)

What other examples can you think of where our way of doing things is not the right way?

The Bible tells us in Proverbs 14:12 (NKJV) and 16:25 (NKJV): *"There is a way that seems right to a man, But its end is the way of death."*

Two of the pigs thought they were doing the right thing by taking shortcuts. Taking shortcuts allowed them to live life to the full. In the end, the big bad wolf destroyed their homes. This is like Matthew 17:26–30 (NKJV): *"And as it was in the days of Noah, so it will be also in the days of the Son of Man: They ate, they drank, they married wives, they were given in marriage, until the day that Noah entered the ark, and the flood came and destroyed them all. Likewise as it was also in the days of Lot: They ate, they drank, they bought, they sold, they planted, they built; but on the day that Lot went out of Sodom it rained fire and brimstone from heaven and destroyed them all. Even so will it be in the day when the Son of Man is revealed."*

The two pigs fared better than the individuals of whom the Bible mentions. The pigs found shelter in their brother's house. The only shelter for man is the blood of Jesus, and few have chosen it.

Comparison 3: Deception

Christians need to be aware of the possibility of deception. We already mentioned one potential example of deception. Consider another one. Maybe dad accepts a promotion at work that he's always wanted. The opportunity seemed good, but it turns out not to be the best choice because he is now working too hard.

We need to know our Bibles so that we can discern God's best for us in all situations. We don't want to be deceived and settle for less.

The wolf deceived the three little pigs, didn't he? We can apply 2 Corinthians 11:14 (NKJV) to their story: *"And no wonder! For Satan himself transforms himself into an angel of light."*

The big bad wolf disguised himself and got a foot in the door of the little pigs' house. The big bad wolf is like Satan, the great deceiver. He can also find his way into our lives. For example, if we harbor sin in our hearts, we can give the devil the open door he's looking for.

That's why we're instructed to remain sober, as 1 Peter 5:8 (NKJV) says: *"Be sober, be vigilant; because your adversary the devil walks about like a roaring lion, seeking whom he may devour."*

I hope you and your family enjoyed this new way of meditating. Really, we can compare the Bible to anything, whether it's children's stories, music, or movies. Again, this gives us another way to meditate on His Word.

Reflection Questions

1. Can you think of other ways to compare *The Three Little Pigs* with the Bible? If so, what verses and principles would you add?

2. How disciplined are you and your family spiritually?

3. What is your favourite way to read the Bible with your family? Do you meditate on a few passages or read an entire chapter in one sitting? What are the advantages and the disadvantages of each?

4. If you or someone you know were questioning their salvation, how would you encourage them?

5. How spiritually sober are you and your family? What are you doing to protect yourself from Satan's attacks?

Chapter 5

CINDERELLA

In the last chapter, we compared the *Three Little Pigs* with the Bible. Now let's do the same with *Cinderella*.

Cinderella is a story about a young woman who lives with her stepmother and stepsisters. The story doesn't mention her father.

The stepmother and stepsisters make Cinderella do all the work for them, although she has little mouse friends to help her. She is dressed in rags, while the stepsisters are well-dressed.

The prince of the land invites all the ladies to a ball. He's looking for a wife. The stepsisters go to the ball. Cinderella is left at home with nothing to wear.

A fairy godmother appears while Cinderella is crying in the garden. The fairy godmother gives Cinderella a fancy dress and glass slippers, turns a pumpkin into her coach and various animals into servants. She goes to the ball and dances with the prince until midnight. The fairy godmother's spell only lasts until then. After that, everything goes back to the way it was. Cinderella leaves the ball in a hurry just before midnight, leaving behind a glass slipper.

The next day, the prince goes in search of the woman who fits the glass slipper. He sends helpers who go from door to door.

The helpers reach Cinderella's house, but her stepsisters lock her in her room. Thankfully, her mouse friends help her escape. She bounds down the stairs and arrives just as the Prince's helpers are leaving. The story ends with Cinderella fitting perfectly into the glass slipper, marrying the prince, and living happily ever after.

Comparison 1: Clothed in Rags

You may already see similarities between *Cinderella* and the Bible. She had a hard life at first, didn't she? As well as not having good clothes, Cinderella lived with a stepfamily that treated her like a slave. They had the latest fashions while she dressed in rags. According to the Bible, so are we before we believe in Christ. Isaiah 64:6 (NKJV) states: *"But we are all like an unclean thing, And all our righteousnesses are like filthy rags; We all fade as a leaf, And our iniquities, like the wind, Have taken us away."*

Likewise, when we believe in Christ, we become new creations. All things become new. 2 Corinthians 5:17 (NKJV) tells us: *"Therefore, if anyone is in Christ, he is a new creation; old things have passed away; behold, all things have become new."*

It's a great deal, but we need to come to Christ to get it. Before Christ, we're like the stepsisters who look nice on the outside but aren't so nice on the inside, at least not in God's eyes.

Comparison 2: There is a Real Enemy

In the story, there is an upcoming ball meant to secure a wife for the prince of the land. He invites everyone, but her stepsisters try to stop Cinderella from attending. They treat her as an enemy, not family. Their actions remind me of Satan, who comes to steal, kill, and destroy. He doesn't want us to know God's blessings. John 10:10 (NKJV) tells us: *"The thief does not come except to steal, and to kill, and to destroy. I have come that they may have life, and that they may have it more abundantly."*

Comparison 3: Wedding

I'm also reminded of the parable in Matthew 22, which compares the Kingdom of Heaven to a wedding feast. Just as Cinderella had to get ready for her ball, so must we be dressed appropriately. Matthew 22:8:9 (NKJV) says: *"Then he said to his servants, 'The wedding is ready, but those who were invited were not worthy. Therefore go into the highways, and as many as you find, invite to the wedding.'"*

Jesus Himself compares natural principles with spiritual ones too, doesn't He?

Comparison 4: We Need a Helper

Remember Cinderella's little helpers, the mice? They're her willing assistants. Believers have something better. We have an invisible Helper in the Holy Spirit. John 14:26 (NKJV) says: *"But the Helper, the Holy Spirit, whom the Father will send in My name, He will teach you all things, and bring to your remembrance all things that I said to you."*

The Holy Spirit also helps us when we're saved. He makes all things new and changes our filthy rags for new ones.

After everyone has gone to the ball, Cinderella is alone, but her fairy godmother pays a visit and saves the day. Christians have something much better than an imaginary fairy godmother. Jesus, through His atonement, understands our grief and is always with us. He's an ever-present help in times of trouble, as Psalm 46:1 (NKJV) tells us: *"God is our refuge and strength, A very present help in trouble."*

Psalm 34:7 (NKJV) is similar, assuring us we have help in troubled times. *"The righteous cry out, and the Lord hears, And delivers them out of all their troubles."*

Comparison 5: Royal Garments

Cinderella only has her royal garments until midnight. When we exchange our filthy rags for Jesus' robes of righteousness, there is no expiration date!

"Then He answered and spoke to those who stood before Him, saying, "Take away the filthy garments from him." And to him He said, "See, I have removed your iniquity from you, and I will clothe you with rich robes." (Zechariah 3:4, NKVJ)

"After these things I looked, and behold, a great multitude which no one could number, of all nations, tribes, peoples, and tongues, standing before the throne and before the Lamb, clothed with white robes, with palm branches in their hands, and crying out with a loud voice, saying, "Salvation belongs to

our God who sits on the throne, and to the Lamb!" (Revelation 4:9–10, NKJV).

Comparison 6: The God Who Seeks

Cinderella's story ends happily, even though she loses her glass slipper at the ball. She doesn't go looking for it. Instead, the prince makes sure that he finds its rightful owner. This reminds me of how Jesus initiates the search for his lost sheep, as told in Luke 15:4-7 (NKJV): *"What man of you, having a hundred sheep, if he loses one of them, does not leave the ninety-nine in the wilderness, and go after the one which is lost until he finds it? And when he has found it, he lays it on his shoulders, rejoicing. And when he comes home, he calls together his friends and neighbours, saying to them, 'Rejoice with me, for I have found my sheep which was lost!' I say to you that likewise there will be more joy in heaven over one sinner who repents than over ninety-nine just persons who need no repentance."*

Comparison 7: Rags to Riches

Speaking of happy endings, those who turn to Christ for salvation have a rag to riches story complete with a much happier ending than Cinderella's. The Bible assures us of this in Revelation 21:4 (NKJV): *"And God will wipe away every tear from their eyes; there shall be no more death, nor sorrow, nor crying. There shall be no more pain, for the former things have passed away."*

We have unpacked a lot in this chapter. Let's review the comparisons we made:

We talked about how Cinderella was dressed in rags. So are we until we believe in Christ.

We talked about Cinderella's enemy, her stepmother and stepsisters. We talked about our enemy, the devil.

We talked about how just as Cinderella needed a proper dress for the ball, so will we. We've all been invited to the Great Feast.

We talked about Cinderella's helpers and our Helper in the Holy Spirit. Just as the mice were always there for her, so is He always there for us. Just as they helped her get ready for the ball, so the Holy Spirit helps us get ready for the Great Feast.

We talked about how Cinderella wore royal clothes, and so will we. The difference is ours doesn't have an expiration date.

Finally, we mentioned that as the prince looked for his princess, so God seeks His children.

Questions for Reflection

1. Can you think of other comparisons between *Cinderella* and the Bible?

2. Are you aware of the ways Satan tries to steal, kill, and destroy in you and your family's lives?

3. Are you and your family aware of God's presence? If not, how can He become more real to you?

4. How have you and your family sensed Jesus' help?

5. How can the knowledge of your happy ending in Christ help you and your family troubled times?

Chapter 6

HANSEL AND GRETEL

We are ready for our third comparison: *Hansel and Gretel.* If you're not familiar with the story, Hansel and Gretel are two children who live with their father and a wicked stepmother. Their stepmother tries to lose them in the woods, but they find their way home. But she's stubborn and keeps trying until she succeeds. The two children get lost in the woods but come across a gingerbread house. They start to eat the gingerbread house when a scary-looking woman opens the door. She invites them inside.

Once inside, she fattens them up with food and gives them beds to sleep in. This is deceptive, as she intends to roast them in the fire and eat them. Eventually, she locks Hansel in a cage and feeds him from there, while Gretel tearfully does the housework. Eventually, Gretel comes up with a plan and pushes the wicked woman into the fire. She and Hansel escape with the woman's jewels and find their father. The stepmother is gone and they live happily ever after.

It's a rather disturbing story, isn't it? Are you already making biblical comparisons?

Comparison 1: Fatherhood

Hansel and Gretel lived with their father and a wicked stepmother. Their father loved them, but he wasn't wise in choosing a new wife. Our Heavenly Father is both wise and loving. Proverbs 2:6 (NKJV) says, *"For the Lord gives wisdom; From His mouth come knowledge and understanding"* and Hosea 1:1 (NKJV) says, *"When Israel was a child, I loved him, And out of Egypt I called My son."*

Comparison 2: Financial Standing

The family is poor. The Bible speaks of those who are poor in spirit. When we recognize our spiritual poverty, we understand our need for Christ, and we're open to the good news of the Gospel.

Matthew 5:3 (NKJV) says: *"Blessed are the poor in spirit, For theirs is the kingdom of heaven."*

Comparison 3: Behaviour and Deception

The wicked stepmother reminds us that, before we believe in Christ, we behave in wicked ways because we are held captive to the will of Satan. See 2 Timothy 2:26 (NKJV): *"...and that they may come to their senses and escape the snare of the devil, having been taken captive by him to do his will."*

The children outsmarted their wicked stepmother's plan to lose them but they stumbled upon the candy-coated house in the woods. Appearances are deceiving, aren't they? The Bible warns believers against deception in James 1:16 (NKJV): *"Do not be deceived, my beloved brethren."*

When Christians read their Bibles, there is less opportunity for deception. It's also important that we remain sober. We already mentioned 1 Peter 5:8 (NKJV) in an earlier chapter.

The owner of the candy-coated house was even worse than the stepmother, although some think the two are the same. Regardless, she planned to feed the children and then eat them. There are many wicked people in the Bible. There are many wicked people today. We know wickedness by its fruit. Psalm 7:14 (NKJV) tells us: *"Behold, the wicked brings forth iniquity; Yes, he conceives trouble and brings forth falsehood."*

Comparison 4: Children

In the end, the children outsmarted the wicked witch, and she met her end. Children are often smarter than we give them credit for. I am reminded of 1 Timothy 4:12 (NKJV): *"Let no one despise your youth, but be an example to the believers in word, in conduct, in love, in spirit, in faith, in purity."*

Comparison 5: Happy Endings

The story ended happily. The children returned to their father with the witches' jewels in their hands. They were no longer poor, and the stepmother was gone. 1 John 4:4 (NKJV) is appropriate: *"You are of God, little children, and have overcome them, because He who is in you is greater than he who is in the world."* So is 1 Samuel 2:7 (NKJV) could also apply: *"The Lord makes poor and makes rich; He brings low and lifts up."*

Reflection Questions

1. Can you think of other comparisons between the Bible and *Hansel & Gretel?*

2. How is your relationship with your father? How does it affect your relationship with your heavenly Father?

3. Can you remember a time when you were poor? How did it affect you?

4. How do you view children? Do hold them in high esteem?

5. What happy endings have you already experienced?

Chapter 7

HUMPTY DUMPTY

Let's shift gears again. Now it's time to compare some nursery rhymes with the Bible. The first is *Humpty Dumpty*.

Humpty Dumpty is a gigantic egg with arms and legs. He's sitting on a ledge and he falls off. None of the kings' men or horses can put him back together again. If you've never heard the rhyme and want to read it word for word, you can find it on the Internet.

Now that we've done some Bible comparisons, I'm sure you can already think of Bible verses that relate to this.

Comparison 1: The Great Fall

Yes, Humpty Dumpty had a big fall. He fell, and he hurt himself. He was so broken that the king's men couldn't put him back together again. Does that sound familiar? Maybe you're thinking what I'm thinking. The great fall rings a bell, doesn't it? For the full story, read Genesis 3.

Humpty Dumpty's fall had serious consequences, but he only hurt himself. The fall of man hand damaged the entire human race.

Sin entered the world with all its consequences. The Bible says that, *"the wages of sin is death"* (Romans 6:23, NKJV). No living person escapes the consequences of sin. But thanks be to God, Jesus died for sin, and all we have to do is believe in His provision. When we do, we're safe. John 3:16 tells us: *"For God so loved the world that He gave His only begotten Son, that whoever believes in Him should not perish but have everlasting life."*

Comparison 2: The King's Men

It sounds like the king's men in the nursery rhyme are part of a royal family, doesn't it? When we believe in Christ, we are royalty, too. You can find this truth in 1 Peter 2:9 (NKVJ): *"But you are a chosen generation, a royal priesthood, a holy nation, His own special people, that you may proclaim the praises of Him who called you out of darkness into His marvellous light."*

There is royalty in the natural as there is in the spiritual, but there is a significant difference. Natural royalty lasts only for this life. Spiritual royalty lasts forever.

Comparison 3: Healing

The king's men couldn't heal Humpty Dumpty. I don't know what methods they used to put him back together again. They must have run out of superglue and duct tape.

Did you know that when someone is hurt in real life, we have the power of the Holy Spirit at our disposal? Yes, Jesus is the Great Physician, but we are His assistants. Did you know that His royal priests - that's us - can also heal? Mark 16:18 (NKJV) says: *"they will take up serpents; and if they drink anything deadly, it will by no means hurt them; they will lay hands on the sick, and they will recover.”*

There is no expiration date on this.. Furthermore, *“Jesus is the same yesterday, today and forever”* (Hebrews 13:8, NKJV).

By the way, this verse isn't saying we should test God by drinking something deadly to prove that it won't harm us. That would be foolish. This verse does mean that healing is available from God through us. Also see James 5:14-16 (NKJV), which says: *“Is anyone among you sick? Let him call for the elders of the church, and let them pray over him, anointing him with oil in the name of the Lord. And the prayer of faith will save the sick, and the Lord will raise him up. And if he has committed sins, he will be forgiven. Confess your trespasses to one another, and pray for one another, that you may be healed. The effective, fervent prayer of a righteous man avails much.”*

Comparison 4: Happy Ending

Humpty Dumpty's story didn't end well. He remained broken. He had no hope. As already discussed in an earlier chapter, believers have a happier ending, and we have hope. Proverbs 23:18 (NKJV) confirms this: *"For surely there is a hereafter, And your hope will not be cut off."*

Reflection Questions

1. Would you add any other comparisons? If so, which Bible verses would you include?

2. How does it make you and your family feel to realize you are part of God's royal priesthood?

3. Do you believe that God's healing power is available today? Have you, your family, or someone you know experienced it?

4. How would you and your family encourage the broken-hearted?

5. How can you remind one another of your hope in Christ?

Chapter 8

JACK & JILL

Jack and Jill is another nursery rhyme. According to the Internet, it has been changed over the years. I remember it like this: two children go up a hill to get water. Jack falls and breaks his crown. Jill follows.

This rhyme isn't uplifting, is it? We'll study what the Bible says to cheer ourselves. If you wanted, you could even create a new nursery rhyme based on what you find in the Bible.

For now, I'm going to give you space to find related Bible verses according to a few comparisons I've thought of. Are you ready?

Comparison 1: Going Up?

Jack and Jill went up the mountain before they went down. If we're Christ's, we'll go to heaven. What verses mention this fact?

Comparison 2: Water

Jack and Jill went to fetch a bucket of water. Before we come to Christ, we're looking for water that will quench our spiritual thirst. Where do you find this principle in the Bible?

Comparison 3: The Fall

We have already talked about the fall of man as recorded in Genesis. Does the Bible mention the fall anywhere else? If so, where?

Comparison 4: The Crown

The crown refers to Jack's head. The Bible also talks about the crown and the head. See how many passages you can find with these two words. Use a tool like Blue Letter Bible.

Comparison 5: Companions

Jill also fell. This reminds us of the importance of

our companions. Do we spend time with those who influence us for good? What does the Bible say about friendship? Find as many verses as you can.

Reflection Questions

1. How did you feel about this exercise?

Chapter 9

BIBLE DRAWINGS

In this chapter, I give you examples of how you could draw Scripture.

Drawing 1

In the first picture, which I drew, the girl is in the middle of the page with all the words mentioned in Philippians 4:8 around her. The words are around her head because these words are what she is thinking about.

You could also draw this verse by drawing things that represent purity, truth, or honour, etc. If you're male, you could draw a man or boy in the middle of the page. You get the idea.

Drawing 2

"...[trust] in the living God, who giveth us richly all things to enjoy;"
I Timothy 6:17b KJV

© Curtis Alexander 2003 - curtis.alexander@sympatico.ca

In the second picture, my husband drew a large gift box with a gift tag that tells us the gift is from Jesus. The box is big because God blesses us abundantly. The man is praising God for the blessings Jesus gives.

You might draw this differently. Your drawing may have a cross to represent Jesus. Surrounding the cross may be some of the things you're praying for. You might draw a bandage to represent healing if that's something you're asking God for

Drawing 3

I drew a lamp to represent the fact that the Bible is a lamp to our feet. You could do the same, but add

feet to the picture, or a path. The choice is yours. These are merely ideas to get you started.

If you want to try drawing Scripture, you're welcome to draw the following passages or choose your own:

John 3:16
Proverbs 17:17
Proverbs 18:21
1 John 4:7
Romans 3:23

If you decide to draw these Scriptures and want to share them with me, you're welcome to email me at jennyalexanderbooks@gmail.com. I'd love to see your creations!

You're also welcome to visit my YouTube channel @art_strings to locate my *Drawing with Jenny* series where I teach the Bible using simple drawings.

Chapter 10

BONUS EXERCISES

In this chapter, you and your family will come up with Scriptures that relate to each drawing. There is no right or wrong answer here.

Drawing 1

Drawing 2

Drawing 3

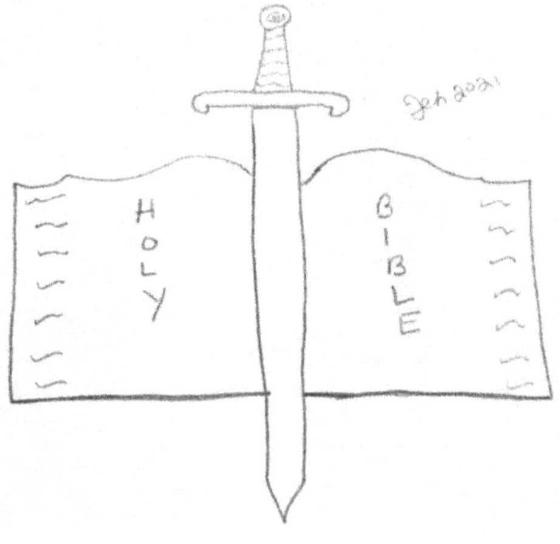

Drawing 4

Drawing 4

Reflection Questions

1. Were you and your family able to think of verses for each drawing?

2. Was the activity challenging or easy?

3. Were you able to find more than one verse for any of the drawings?

4. Have you thought of drawing your own pictures and coming up with verses? This would be like Bible Pictionary.

 5. Have you thought of other ways to meditate on the Bible that weren't discussed in this book?

Chapter 11

REFERENCES & RESOURCES

https://www.alltopeverything.com/top-10-best-selling-books-of-all-time/

BlueLetterBible.org

Curtis Alexander's YouTube channel:
https://www.youtube//@CurtisAlexandermusic

Foxe's Christian Martyrs. Abridged Christian Classics.

Fulton, Richard. Genesis to Jesus Facebook group: https://www.facebook.com/groups/196422091306233

Hickey, Marilyn. (2013). Seeing Jesus. Bible Encounter. A life-transforming walk from Genesis to Revelation - seeing Jesus in every book of the Bible.

Jenny Alexander

Knowimsaved.com

66

Water. (2004). AMGs Encyclopedia of Bible Facts.

Epilogue

Thank you for reading Imaginative Bible Meditations: Strengthening Family Devotions with Creativity.

I hope you've enjoyed learning more about what biblical meditation can look like. We can draw Scripture or do word and topical studies. We can compare the natural with the spiritual. We can "interview" Jesus or other Bible characters. In short, there is no wrong way to study and meditate on the Bible, as long as we're rightly dividing the Word of Truth.

Before we say good-bye, may I ask you to leave me a short written review on Amazon? Reviews mean so much and help others find my book.

Connect with Me

If you'd like to connect, visit my Facebook author page (Jenny Alexander, Author) via Facebook.com/hopefortheheartbroken

or visit my blog:
https://jennyswordsofworth.blogspot.com/

Acknowledgments

Thank you, as always, to my husband, Curtis. Your encouragement and support is truly amazing.

Thank you, GetCovers, for the amazing cover design.

Thank you, Paige Spear, for your wonderful feedback and editing. Your suggestions and belief in my book gave me the confidence to move forward with publishing it.

Thank you, Richard Fulton's, for your ministry and your website knowimsaved.com. Your teaching gave me a solid Bible foundation.

Thank you to the Medium writing platform which helped me gain confidence as a writer.

Thank you, Jasmine Womack, for your 5-day challenge on Facebook which continues to help me with the publishing process.

About the Author

Jenny has a story to tell. Her story is one of recovery and hope. Though her unhealthy first marriage ended in divorce, she healed and now thrives. She writes to help others recover from divorce and make better choices when it comes to relationships.

She is a happy housewife and author who lives in Ontario with her husband, Curtis. She loves pursuing creative interests like sketching, playing the violin, and writing. She holds a Masters in Human Services Counselling from Liberty University.

Books by This Author

Divorce Recovery Handbook: Effective Strategies for Healing

Stop Settling When It Comes to Love: Wise Dating Practices for Women

On the Road to Recovery: Overcoming 10 Common Speed Bumps Post-Divorce

Breaking Free from Toxicity: A Relationship Evaluation Guide

Assurance for Your Soul: A Collection of Original Christian Poetry

Jenny has also written word searches, activity books, journals, children's books, and books about self-publishing and plans to release other books in the future.